D0879016

Of Time & Toronto by Raymond Souster

This book was published with the assistance of the Canada Council, the Ontario Arts Council and others. We acknowledge the support of the Canada Council for the Arts for our publishing program.

Typesetting and design by Michael Macklem

Printed in Canada

PUBLISHED IN CANADA BY OBERON PRESS

For Rosalia, my Susi, as always, and to the memory of

Richard Woollatt (1931-1998)
Harry Iddon (1910-1999)
& Donald Thornton (1923-1999)
"If you are out to describe the truth, leave elegance to the tailor" — Albert Einstein.

Printed in Canada

PUBLISHED IN CANADA BY OBERON PRESS

Death, Bus Shelter; Go Touch Timothy; Black Trillium; Bloor-Danforth Subway Car; Mike White at the Westover; In Praise of the Small Bakers; More Violence on the Picket Line; High Park Cross-Country Run; Action Central.

John Brown Leads a Raid on Harpers Ferry.

Personal Notes

PRELUDE

To die
just before a summer's dawn,
when a first song-sparrow
achieves his opening trills
thinly tremulous.

STILL ALIVE

Snow-crispness under my feet,
west wind slamming at my cheeks,
warm sun through the icicle morning
stabbing at my half-shut eyes;

with children slithering over ice,
hockey sticks slashing out in time
to their ear-splitting cries.

How much more than this
do I need to tell me
I am still alive?

GRAVEYARD SHIFT

Five o'clock and still sleepless,
with eyelids half-shuttered,
I am still commanded
to remain here at my desk,

awaiting the late arrival
of the last two lines
of what's turning out to be
a reluctant, foot-dragging
little bitch of a poem.

TO NO-ONE IN PARTICULAR

Remember what old Satchel said?
"Each time I look over my shoulder
something seems to be gaining on me."

I don't know about yours
but my damn thing always stays well back,
walking, running at the same even pace,
except for the odd, unexpected time
he speeds up or slows down
just the slightest bit,
to mimic my footsteps, I suppose,
much like the heartless pet owner
who tightens or slackens the leash
of his frolicsome dog.

O that manner of his,
so cool, so very much in control,
is more than enough to make me wish
that the race was over, once and for all;
with all the time in the world then
to test the strange, new-found sweetness
of total defeat, absolute surrender!

DAYS

When I hit a bad day
I'm lower than a through-the-mails assassin.
Then, when a good day comes dancing
from somewhere right out of the blue,
I'm up there stacked solid for hours,
above the highest, most comfortable clouds.

THE WRITING GAME

Stay wide awake,
keep moving your pencil
across the page.

Until the saviour dawn
in its majesty lays bare
the utter folly of the word.

REVIEWING STAND, LATE FALL

Through the blue haze
of this late-autumn afternoon,
my dogged leaf battalions
straggle by for their last inspection.

I give each one of them
my snappiest five-finger
farewell salute,
as their march of death begins.

A DOCTOR'S BEST ADVICE TO
AN OLDER PATIENT

Very early to rise, even later to bed —
you'll have so much fun you won't know you're dead!

BIG OLD MONSTER CROW

Whatever that big old monster crow
wanted to tell me the other day,
I wasn't in any mood to listen,
especially from a rude, noisy bird.

But today, when I feel more ready
for whatever his message is,
damning or otherwise,
he seems to have left the neighbourhood,
and where he's got to no-one knows,
could be easily a dozen miles away
as any crowbird flies.

So, my great jet-black,
wind-shaking goony bird,
please come back very soon,
and I'll give you my solemn promise
that I'll listen with the greatest attention
to every single, solitary word
coming out of your raucous, salivating throat,
no matter what you have in mind for me.

Now we've watched the days slip by,
and the welcome, flapping sound
of your wings hasn't been heard
from any swaying tree-top, doesn't blacken
any corner of the local sky
that my eyes can fathom,
big old crowbird, we're truly something
of a queer pair, you and I!

ANYTHING YOU SAY, COACH

Remember, keep your chin up, boy,
so this lousy world can quickly floor you
with a fast, dirty knockout punch.

FACT

It's hard to find anyone
whose life doesn't touch
or alter another life,
even in the slightest way.

If you do meet such a person,
he'll probably turn out to be
a frustrated poet or the next leader
of Her Majesty's Loyal Opposition.

14

THE SAME SAD OLD STORY

At age twenty-three
widely touted as poetry's
latest whiz-kid wonder.

Now at seventy- six and counting,
finally pegged, neatly pigeon-holed,
as an all but forgotten,
all too human blunder.

BLESSING

My late-evening surprise —
unknown perfumes of passionate flowers
rub against me as I open
our squeaky back screen-door,
step out slowly
into night's dark salvation
unfolding.

FACING UP

Your old friend the calendar
reminds you with its knowing grin
that today you've finally reached
that big plateau of seventy-five.
Think of it — how many years,
months, weeks and days,
all flushed too quickly down the drain —
before you realized at last
that at the best of times
(count them on two fingers)
you were only barely half-alive!

FINALE

If this late-spring morning
were the last one allowed me,
I'd go out shouting to the heavens
my loudest song in praise

of intimate bird chatter,
of bluebells running riot
through solemn garden beds,
of one darkened shadow
of a bird's wing
(fleeting as an eye-wink)
across sunlit grass,
with madcap squirrels streaking after.

S.O.B.

I've been called an S.O.B.
probably a few more times
than the average citizen.

But I have to admit
I was totally unprepared,
I was even slightly shocked
when, after being whisked
to St. Joe's last night
in an ambulance, face-mask in place,
and sucking hard
on a good old oxygen bottle,

to find it there plain as day
on my copy of the out-patient's
emergency-room admittance form,
right under the heading
Patient's Complaint,
those damning typed-in initials
(you've guessed it!)
S.O.B.

Very definitely he's turned out to be
a person never to be trusted —
least of all by himself.

SOME LINES FOR JOE

Joe Spring, if you're still alive,
and somehow read this,

come back again
with the little toy shovel
you swung in anger that day
we played together,
me six, you five,
in the dump on the south side
of the street quaintly called Indian Grove.

I still have a small scar
beside my right eye, Joe,
but I've never held a grudge
since that day in '27.

So come back today, Joe,
if you happen to be around,
and don't forget to bring
your old toy shovel with you —

it may not be too late
to drive some sense
into my still-stubborn head!

Neighbourhoods

WINTER AT THE END
OF SAND BEACH ROAD

Eleven, twelve, maybe thirteen ducks
(who con count straight on this wind-whipper
of a day?)

by some miracle survive
dip and plunge of each onshore wave,
and, what's more, seem to thrive on it,

as the wind and waves combine,
old hands at this tricky game,
try again and again so patiently
to flip those bobbing corks right over,

with no end in sight
to this dazzling, daredevil struggle,
fought out on this sullen-faced
Lake Ontario afternoon.

THE THIRTEENTH DAY OF CHRISTMAS

Green, still defiant
corpses of the Christmas trees,
their needles strewn like barbs
through the glistening snow,

waiting for the garbage truck,
screech of its wheels
their one short burial cry.

BY THE DAY OF THE ELECTION

By the day of the election
I'd become so depressed
that I went out and voted
for the local Liberal candidate!

ON BABY POINT ROAD

For the record only —
an event of great importance
to all who know this street
has gone completely unnoticed.

This then is just to say
that Wanda's brave magnolia bush
greeted this morning's sun
with three most delicate
cup-shaped flowers.

Worth more, I'd say,
than the collective weight
of every house in this neighbourhood
built of ages-old
Humber Valley limestone,

hauled (so the story goes),
up the Baby Point cliffs
by a dozen profusely sweating,
ill-tempered elephants.

A CHARACTER IN SEARCH OF AN AUTHOR

Trying to find Michael's house
in this Don Mills springtime maze,
is proving more difficult, more puzzling
than *Coming through Slaughter.*

NO SURRENDER

One black, bewildered spider
trying calmly, patiently to climb
the smooth, sheer, shining slope
of our ancient, empty bathtub.

Give it up, old thing,
I want to tell him or her,
you'll never make it, believe me,
in a month of Mondays.

But he/she either doesn't hear
or, more likely, can't be bothered
to pay me the slightest time of day,
keeps on sliding, slipping, slithering,
but never stops coming on,
always ready for another brave try
at the plainly impossible!

SHOWDOWN

Those impossible crows again,
this morning, early.

Bitching, black punks of Satan,
who's running this universe,
you or me?

CHANCE MEETING IN THE DENTIST'S OFFICE

"If you must know, I was a green two-pipper
in the Australian infantry's Sixth Div.
First they shot us up to Egypt,
where we arrived just in time to join
an Indian Div. and a Polish Army Corps,
with the sweet job of keeping rampaging Rommel
from breaking out across that desert hell.

"Then, of course, just days before
the real big show at El Alamein,
the lot of us were shipped to Italy,
landing at Taranto, then slugging our way north,
until we reached the Appenines.
There someone got the bright idea
I was the best bloke to join the Partisans,
good fighters, I soon found out,
if properly led, and though armed at the best
with old World War One rifles,
had to wait patiently
until a comrade dropped by their side
to finally get a weapon they could fight with.

"Then one day, quite by chance,
I saw the sight of any lifetime —
Benito and his mistress strung up,
then left hanging there upside down
in the great square of Milan —
at least that's who they said they were,
there wasn't enough left of either face
so you could be absolutely sure."

SUMMER DAY DEEP IN LANGMUIR WOOD

Sepulchre-cool
is the closest
I can come to it,
and eerie, perhaps,
like that lake could never manage.

STORM CASUALTY

In our neighbours' backyard,
thirty feet from our door,
its frantic cries drowned out
by a storm that lashed and ripped
everything in its way all night —

now revealed in sober daylight,
completely helpless, awkwardly lying
on one cracked side,
my shining-green plastic
(spout sunshine-yellow),
one-litre watering-can.

SKUNKED AGAIN

Right at the very worst moment
of my wife's sleep-shattering,
5 AM angina attack,

I sniff the all-too-familiar
calling card of Sammy Skunk,
luckily manage to close all doors and windows
before my wife gets even a whiff
(a small miracle right there).

Hours later I still imagine
somewhere down our long driveway
or out in the backyard shadows,
Sammy running over in his mind
what he might have said to me:

"I even knocked twice, old sport,
but you never answered me;
that was shortly before we tried out
our new, all-purpose fragrence
as a first in this neighbourhood,
as I knew you certainly
didn't want to be left out.

"Never mind, I'll call around again,
perhaps some night next week,
at which time I hope you'll be receptive
to what could easily prove to be
a snootful of a real surprise.
Cheers, now. Your old friend, Sammy."

FLY-PAST

One goose-gaggle in a hurry
sweeps by at minimum treetop level
through the steadily-greying dusk of Baby Point,
shouts of command ringing out, re-echoing above;

with me deciding quickly that it has to be
a pathfinder squadron well ahead of main force,
but kept bang on course, safe from harm,
by the master navigators out there on either flank,
whose honks of direction lead this daring band
spread out above across the sky.

And I can easily picture this flight
pressing on through the last hurried miles
to their first co-ordinate,
one more checkpoint thankfully arrived at
before heading due south across the inky waters
of our own broad Lake Ontario.

No doubt using the very same flight-plan
that their fathers, grandfathers used,
while I'm left behind, reflecting as I go
through my yard picking up dead branches
from the half-frozen ground, that it's going to take
all the early green grass we can muster
to show through next March's snow and ice,
needing more than a few stiff blasts
of warm air lifting their wings,
to bring these wanderers back in time
to greet the happy sun, their boisterous cries
all but drowning out the unseen throb
of their matchless wings!

SNOW-SQUALLS, MID-FEBRUARY

People on an early-winter evening
as they hurry past our house,
are bent over, hunched up,
as if to fight the wind
rudely flicking its ice-darts
of freezing snowflakes
into every brave face there;
even those who try turning their backs
to escape at least some of the onslaught,
are forced finally to admit defeat,
slithering, sliding on the ice-mirrored pavements;
give a last shrug-up inside their coats,
before facing head-on chilled fingers
clutching at every throat.

No wonder when I finally turn away
from this warm, snow-streaked window lookout,
my shoulders feel hunched over too,
while my back seems to harbour
most unusual stabs of pain,
as if I'd only just come inside
from battling the two-and-change gusty blocks
from the nearest Jane Street bus-stop.

29

FERNS' WORLD

In the coolest corner of our garden,
between the straggly bushes
and the fancy new six-footer
of a fence built by my neighbour,

I found entirely by chance
the dozen ferns
of a tiny world all its own,
thriving through that hot and dusty June.

I'm sure you wouldn't have thought
this random discovery of mine
the small, wondrous miracle I made it,
or marvelled at how each delicate frond reached up,
so green, so perfect-patterned,
it was more than enough to take breath straight away.

That's perhaps why I've waited so long
before finally fashioning this poem,
not willing, I'm sure,
to share such a precious secret
with anyone not caring
even half as much as I did.

So you few who read this now,
please don't reveal what I've said,
better still, perhaps entirely forget
that you chanced on this very private page.

PARACHUTE SCHOOL

One more leaf
must drift down
with graceful ease,

before we close up
our special parachute-school
for treetop candidates,
after another smooth-sailing
record-breaking year.

"RAGS, BONES & BOTTLES"

How, in my dream tonight, they rode again
down that laneway at Ulster and Bathurst Streets,
their high, piercing, almost unrecognizable cries
of "Rags, Bones, Bottles" always heard before
the squeaks, the rattling squeals
of their mostly empty peddlers' waggons
came finally into view,
each bearded, venerable ancient man
(or so we kids thought them),
dressed in slightly soiled and dusty
black, shiny hats and long black frock-coats,
as they gently urged on their tired,
skin-and-bone ugly,
patient, fly-plagued horses,
stopping only when a Bathurst Street kid
opened his garden's laneway door
to offer up his pile of *Stars* and *Telys*,
or half a dozen large and small pop bottles,
then waited while the old long-bearded one,
high on his waggon, came up with his price
(two or three cents usually,
very seldom as high as a nickel),
then held out the open palm
of their hand to receive the big, cool coppers,
counted out one by one
by the sweating driver bending down;
then, with a quick flip of the reins,
the old man, the horse, the squeaky waggon
would rattle on up the lane toward Harbord Street.

And with their trade now done,
and before those waggons had moved
too far up the lane, we kids,
usually two or three of us together,
and with our courage being put to the test,
would shout out at the top of our voices
"Sheenie, Sheenie, Sheenie,"
which was what a regular guy
was supposed to do
unless he was a sissie,
a poor softy like me.

UPSIZING

The corner drug addict,
nose dripping, unshaven,
has eyes that look strangely far away,
holds out a dirty plastic cup
to collect what he's sensed will be
his next easy handout of the day.

In a good mood, I drop a looney in,
and the guy makes my day
when he says strictly deadpan:
"Another afternoon like this
and I can make a move up
to a real tin cup."

That's free enterprise for you,
most of us probably would say
to ourselves as we hurried on.

But then, on the other hand,
I wonder if perhaps I've missed
his message altogether.

"BURNS COAL BURNS BEST"

In those years of the terrible Thirties
you burned either coal or coke
in the sturdy family furnace,
with the Sousters burning coal,
the cheapest anthracite, from Pennsylvania.

The arrival of a coal truck on Indian Grove
was the nearest thing to an event
that ever took place there,
unless you wanted to count
the daily visits of the Lake Simcoe ice-truck,
the iceman's tongs firmly gripping
a shiny, twenty-five-pound block
of ice, leaving a long, wet trail
up our steep, narrow side-drive.

The coal came in dusty, bulging sacks,
each weighing a hundred pounds or so,
and carried from the back of the truck
up our steep-sloping driveway
(our house, like all its neighbours,
built on an excuse for a hill)
to the last cellar window, open now,
where the bags were hefted with a crash
into the empty basement coal-bin,
the two grimy coalmen
bending over so far with their load
that you wondered how they ever kept their balance
half as well as they always seemed to do.

At the inquisitive age of eight
I knew that a ten-ton load meant
that each coalman carried on his back
about a hundred bags each,
often through rain or, worse, snow,
up slopes or down them, those cat-footed men.

Coalmen were usually in their forties, fifties,
short. wiry, small-built, silent types,
each dust-stained, Al-Jolson-like face
lacking only the thick-painted
white oval of a mouth,
along with shining teeth that obligingly gleamed.

If the weather at the time was very hot,
my mother usually made a special point
of carrying out to each thirsty coal-slinger
a glass of her special, ice-cold lemonade.
That was the least we could do, my mother said,
for these men with their sweaty,
grimy line of work.

And right here I remember once
my father cutting in with: "And let's not forget
that it's honest work that has to be done
by someone or all our houses
will be pretty uncomfortable
on those cold fall and winter nights."

36

And, warming to the subject, he went on:
"That's also why your mother and I
are sacrificing in every way we can
to give you and your brother
the best schooling available,
so you'll never have to carry
dirty bags of coal to dump
in peoples' coal-bins;
we'd never want you dirty to the skin
from being covered with the coal- and coke-dust
of this miserable, dead-end job."

FIRST FROST

Yesterday in this half of the garden
perhaps nine or ten crinkly, yellowed leaves,
now today perhaps another twenty more.

With the way things are going at the moment,
unless we reach someone big enough
to call a prompt halt to all this dying,
there's no telling how soon we'll all be faced
with the rampaging ruin of another year.

CHRISTIANNE AND THE SQUIRREL

In a dream last night
my soul-sister Christianne spoke to me:
"That electric conductor of a squirrel,
which yesterday I had the urge to draw,
right after he'd scooted head-first down
the oak tree right outside my window,
came back today — a small, darting miracle.

"And as he sat munching
my first piece of stale white bread,
he started talking in his bold, charming way:
'Lady, this life's the pits,
and I don't mean the Christie Street kind,
but I like you, so don't disappoint me,
as most of you humans I've met with do —
all right, if you want to draw me, I'm available,
which means get your blackest sketching-pencil out,
and make sure you catch all the seriousness
shining at the back of my eyes,
which you might easily miss
as you watch me going through
my scamper-ass routine.'"

And my soul-sister Christianne continued
with the rest of it:
"My new friend was good enough to wait
through two more white-bread offerings,
while I sketched him in this tree
with familiar neighbourhood background —
stately old houses with their chimneys
mixed with stubby high-rise intruders;
the latter, though still blocks from here,
are sure to force their ugliness in time
on these easygoing, unsuspecting streets.

"There, my dear squirrel's gone again,
but now at least I've given him
a meaningful place
in the master plan of my world."

TWO GREAT SWANS, GRENADIER POND

Certainly we're getting older now
(our slowly-rusting-to-death
1985 Pontiac Acadian
all the proof you need,
if there's any doubt);

which makes it more comforting today
to be driving west on the Queensway Extension,
and, stopped by the red light at Ellis Avenue,
to have what seems
a long, thirty-second look
at the south end of Grenadier Pond,
as it rests in mid-March with a coating
of fresh glare ice
covering the whole expanse of it,
except behind a new, man-made breakwall
where open water laps and ebbs steel-grey.

And where, precisely as if on cue,
in this iron emptiness of an afternoon —
look there: unexpectedly, a great white swan
makes an effortless arrival, and head held high,
slowly waddles forward as her majesty
carefully inspects this corner
of her pond-wide kingdom,
who I see at this very moment is being joined
by what must be her consort, a second great swan
of dazzling whiteness, arriving
with a sliding, timid gait,
not helped by stumbling feet.

It's easy to imagine him
muttering something about the utter foolishness
of most short-cuts, while still managing to keep
neck proudly erect, the puffed-up feathers
still nobly held.
                    Unluckily for me,
my stoplight now flashes green,
leaving me no choice at all
but to go with the flow, as they say,
which means an exchanging
of this peaceful parkside scene
(linked so closely to my child-years, my youth, my manhood)
for the clogged, noisy line of cars ahead,
each exhaust-pipe belching steadily
as it pours blue wreaths of choking fumes
into the city's dying, golden-sunset air!

41

Outside World

EASTER, 1993

In the night a Jew
knifed by Palestinians;
a Palestinian cut down
by Israeli patrols.

Twenty years from today
someone may read this poem,
ask what it was all about.

Among the people gathered,
only a handful, if that,
will have any answer.

GROUNDED EAGLES

Per ardua ad astra

Even at Manning Pool, Toronto,
the new recruits in blue
of midsummer '41
found there were two air forces —

the lucky guys who were going to fly
with the white band in their caps,
and the rest of us, grounded eagles,
slated for lonely Prairie training-schools
or even more remote home-war runways
spread across our two-ocean graveyard.

45

FLY

Find a way to tap the energy
exploding from this single
frantic, buzz-mad fly,

and I'll promise you you'll keep
every last turbine turning
should our proud Niagara
ever run close to dry.

FOR THE THIRTY-SIXTH PARLIAMENT OF CANADA

One timid foot forward,
two cautious steps back.

I suppose a Nelson or Napoleon
is what we really lack.

46

NOW WHENEVER SOMEONE SAYS YOUR NAME: A RECOLLECTION

In memoriam Ralph Gustafson

Ralph, now whenever someone says your name,
or it's quoted in some literary review,
I've been taken back in memory more than once
to that Hades-hot August evening rush-hour
(how hot was it? Would you believe
even New York cabbies were in miserable moods!)
when Lia and I took an airless taxi
across town from La Guardia,
first through the shimmering sweat-box that was Queen's,
then into the twice-dead, breathless Manhattan canyons,
ending up in front of a faded hotel marquee,
which the ad in last week's *Globe* had hooked us
with its cunning phrase, "right in the very heart
of picturesque Gramercy Park."

Well, granted it may have been picturesque
circa 1910; but now as the oppressive
near-dusk was thankfully lowering,
and we walked into our hotel and across the lobby,
I'm sure the first faint alarm bells
must have sounded inside us. Nevertheless,
we checked in without any trouble at the desk,
then followed a bellhop carrying our bags
onto an elevator, which reeked of disinfectant,
and slowly clicked off the floors to the eighth,
where we were introduced to a dimly lit hallway,
with our bellhop stopping halfway down and selecting
a door with an indistinct number that unlocked for him,
us waiting while he dumped our bags on the floor,

then clicked on the lights as we stood in the doorway
with unbelieving looks as the first whiffs of a strong musty
    odour
laced with antiseptic spray struck our unprotected senses,
smacking us squarely first in the nose,
then the eyes, which met the dark-green wallpaper
smeared with oil and grease stains much too prominent
for even the half-dark of this room to hide.

It couldn't have taken us more than a long ten minutes
after we'd paid off the bellhop and were alone,
to vote thumbs down on this miserable excuse for a room,
with Lia almost right away saying, Look, I don't think I can
    stand
being in here for another hour, never mind the whole night;
and she didn't need to say one word more, I'd become
as convinced as her that we'd drawn a real lemon.
Then I'd better get busy on the blower
before it gets any later, I said,
but struck a snag right away,
there was no yellow-pages book in our room,
only the huge four-inch regular monster. So, I remember,
I had to leave Lia there alone, go down, grab a phone in
    the lobby,
under "Hotel" finding pages of listings, making it
a real crap shoot. So for the next fun-filled hour
everyone I talked to sounded very nice, very patient,
only it seems there were several large conventions in town,
so each place was booked solid, some for longer than a week.
I finally put down the phone, wondering how Lia'd take the
    news
when I went back to our lousy room. But right about then
I had my one break of the day. Your name, Ralph,
for some reason flashed brightly on my radar screen.
You still might be in New York, I reasoned, remembering now

48

how I'd tried to phone you in '46, when Bill Goldberg and I
had hit the Big Apple on a shoe-string weekend,
with Louis Dudek's one-roomed
Amsterdam-and-125th-Street apartment
all ours for a three-day flop.
I believe you were listed
under a Central Park South location then,
but your telephone rang and rang
and nobody answered. So I never had the pleasure
of meeting you. Now it was 1952,
and here I was ringing you again.

Hoping against hope that someone would answer,
so you might somehow pull off a miracle for us,
I said inside, Thank the Lord, as you finally answered,
your calm, even voice reassuring from the start.
Next, I tried to shorten our tale of woe,
but still must have talked your ear off.
That's rotten luck, Ray, you said. It's pretty late, I know,
but there's got to be something available
in a big town like this. Just let me get back to you,
and relax, I'll do the worrying for a while.

So, feeling much relieved, I rode the elevator back up,
told a nervous wife (who'd been wondering where I'd got to)
that you'd gone to work for us,
and if anyone could find a room at this hour
our poet friend with his B.I.S.* background
would be sure to snare something somewhere.

And, wonder of wonders, less than half an hour later,
our phone rang suddenly, making us jump in our chairs.
It was you, Ralph, telling us we were in luck,
you'd lassooed us a nice room up at the Great Western,
a hotel Jack Dempsey'd once owned, right next

to the Carnegie Hall rehearsal rooms.
I think you'll like it, I've stayed there myself,
so pack up your things,
I told them you'd be there in an hour.

And not that much later the two of us were admiring
the huge, high-ceilinged room on the fourth floor
of our great new hotel. Still marvelling
at the monster hulk of a bathtub
raised four inches off the floor, with the world's
largest hot and cold running faucets. And I lost no time,
    Ralph,
in phoning you back to stammer out our heartfelt thanks,
and of course with my big mouth flapping simply had to tell
    you
of our elevator ride as we checked out
of our Gramercy Park disaster. The elevator man
looked surprised to see us leaving (or was he?),
and told us quite matter-of-factly
about the fellow Canadian ("from Toronto like you"),
murdered in his room earlier that afternoon.
It seems he'd brought a stranger back with him,
got fatally stabbed for his stupidity.
I still recall your words, Ralph: "it's a good thing
you got out of there tonight. Now I hope you'll feel
like joining me for lunch tomorrow;
if you both eat Oriental food,
there's a great place down in the Village."

50

Words we could expect, I suppose,
from our saviour of the moment,
our friend forever after. Your many kindnesses
have stayed with us and warmed us,
are even warmer in our hearts today.
Ralph, we wish you somehow could have lived forever!

*British Information Service

51

THAT ICEBERG OFF ST. JOHN'S

Luckily, as it happened,
coming back to our living-room
as the TV began to flash
the final minute of the CBC's
eleven-o'clock evening news,

and catching, with the luck of the Irish,
the last few precious seconds
of an amateur camera-shoot
captured earlier in the day
by a wide-awake guy in St. John's,

who for some reason had his camera
trained dead ahead on the entrance
to the harbour they call
with good reason "the Narrows,"
and, amazed, saw gliding by
in all deliberate majesty,
Pratt's ageless iceberg
through the tall cliffs' opening,

looking sparkling and pure,
in what must have been
the early-morning sunshine
out especially to cheer on
the lonely, ghostly voyager.

THE CHILD AND HUNGER

While one single child
cries himself to sleep
from unpardonable hunger,

each one of us carries
that child's belly-pains
in some part of our gut.

THE SERBS HAVE THIS SAYING

Never think of quitting the fight
while there are still enough
noble warriors left
to bury your dead.

IN OLD ST. PETER'S

Fourteen newly consecrated bishops sprawled
on silken stomachs before their Pope.
Enough to make a Buddha force back a smile,
a battered Christ to finally give up hope.

IRON MAN, MIRACLE MAN

In the camera shoot before tonight's
all-star baseball game,
that great White Sox reliever, Roberto Hernandez,
in one crazy movement,
that's all over in a frantic split-second,
loses his balance standing on a platform
where the AL team photo is being taken,

and, lashing out to save himself,
smashes his forearm
into the face of his neighbour, Cal Ripken,
giving him an instant bloody, broken nose;

which of course has the reporters in the stands
running around like decapitated chickens,
with all the buzz plainly centred
on whether the great Ripken streak
is finally about to be broken.

But, precisely at game-time,
slightly bandaged up and sedated,
our Iron Man, without noticeable trouble,
takes his usual place at short
in the starting lineup of the AL favourites,
and in case there's anyone who needs reminding,
it's Ripken's fourteenth All-Star appearance,
with him starting in a couple of minutes
his 2239th consecutive game,
and it's equally true that he's played
through many worse times and nights than this,
with a mind-set so tempered by the years
he's ready for many more of them.

And, game over, I can easily imagine him
(if he's in a rare mood, that is),
quipping with the press —
"Hey, boys, you don't double out the runners
with your nose, use it tripling off the wall,"

and he makes them believers forever
as they crowd around baseball's Miracle Man.

AND NOW OUR FIRST WOMAN PRIME MINISTER

They're calling her
"Queen for a Day."

Actually (if you'll pardon that word),
there may not be an election
for another eighty days.

Surely time enough to allow
her tiara to fit more snugly.

56

THREE DAYS WENT BY

Three days went by
before that first knock on his door,
another two days after that before
they got the landlord with his key.

It's not recorded who screamed first,
or who made it fastest to the john,
or who finally cut him down.

Some say it was an ill-advised
last attempt to get human attention
for an unknown, out-of-work actor-poet,

if so it failed miserably,
taking almost two more days
to get proper ID, and, to top it off,
both Montreal papers got his name wrong.

Very fittingly, as it turned out,
the second -biggest loser
was his pinch-penny landlord.
This totally unannounced last act, last scene
of a sad, pathetic drama,
cost him three weeks' back rent,
with the added aggravation
of having to take
five dollars a week less,
for that white-elephant of a room
that held onto his late tenant's death-stink,
never let it go completely away.

TO THE COCKROACHES OF THE AIRMEN'S MESS

No. 4 Repair Depot, Scoudouc, NB, 1944

I still fondly remember
how in a very short time
we became good friends,
first you with us,
then more gradually we with you.
You never once seemed afraid,
while we airmen still had qualms about you,
being shy, very uptight Canadians.
But even this didn't stop us,
first at breakfast, then at lunch and supper,
from saving you some left-over scraps,

watching with much amusement
as you crawled out from underneath the table,
once we'd signalled that we'd finished eating
by noisily pushing back our wooden benches.
Many times you were barely able
to make it across our table-top,
scraping swollen, stuffed stomachs,
grossly overweight legs,
but still proudly going through the motions,
just for us,

dragging away our rather sad table-leavings
in a show of thankfulness that never wavered;
and then made it more than doubly clear

that in that upside-down world
the real enemy was not Private Mussolini
or even Little Corporal Hitler,
but, much more greatly feared, our timeless enemies,
bringing endless ache to the belly,
desolation crushing the soul,
all from mad Sister Hunger,
her idiot Brother Famine,
and, close behind,
ghoul-faced Cousin Drought,
all members of the Devil's inner band!

NEW YEAR NOTE

In this Year of the Rat
already the mice
seem to be getting big ideas.

THIS POET OF SARAJEVO

This poet of Sarajevo
is burning, very reluctantly,
one book at a time,
the 5000 volumes
of his long-cherished library,
in a desperate effort
to keep his family warm.

Today he begins with Dostoievsky,
then gets a real blaze going
with a fat, prized *Ulysses*,
next comes *To the Lighthouse*,
and so on it goes . . . .

He's hoping he'll have some volumes left
by the time winter's over.
"I'm throwing my own books on last,"
he says with a grin,
admitting without any shame
the vanity of poets
whether living, dying
or merely freezing slowly
one toe and finger at a time.

TEN CENTS A BUNCH

Poems, ten cents a bunch,
good gentlemen, who'll buy?

At least the answer's quick —
not in a stinking pig's eye!

61

THE STONES OF MATAPEDIA

Forty stones more or less
and a silver key to God knows what,
sit inside the lid
of a little cardboard box
on my crowded writing-table.

It has to be at least twenty years
since Ron helped me choose them
from a much larger, fuller box
in his Côte St.-Luc rooftop apartment,
relating how he'd picked them up
so carefully one summer's day,
along the banks
of that foaming-mad, river-rush
called Matapédia.

"Treat them with care, Ray,
as you would precious grandchildren,
and they'll last you a lifetime," he told me.

So far long past your own life,
Ron Everson,
and waiting there now for me.

What's your best guess, Ron —
does a stone a month
sound about right?

FOR EARLE

It seemed you never stopped
long enough to put any meat
on those bones of yours,
you became the Road Runner,
reborn to leave us
far behind in your dust.

I remember you as generous,
especially toward the young,
fiercely loyal to the act of poetry,
and striving always
for something just out of reach.

Now with you safely under ground,
the downsizers can begin
their gleeful distortions.

Your answer, Earle?
I feel I can almost catch
the proud, scornful echo of your voice:
"Try downsizing this!"

63

THE GREATEST POET IN THE WORLD

In this sand-scratch of time,
April 1997,
there's only one real contender,
Cid Corman, aged 70-plus,
formerly of Boston, Massachusetts,
but for many years now
a transplanted citizen
of Kyoto, Japan.

As to backing up this claim,
let me quote from his most recent letter:
I have 20,000 unpublished,
perfectly publishable poems
in this room alone
(I don't exaggerate, alas),
apart from a dozen full-length books.
I don't have the time, the energy or the means
even to throw them at publishers;
in fact, I don't have time
to look at the books after writing them,
already lost in other work.
And this tiny room
I call my "Little Chaos":
books, papers from floor to ceiling,
and hard enough even to seat myself
at this desk, a large desk,
but with hardly space
for my small typewriter.

"As I may have scribbled on a postcard,
I write a book of poems *every day*
(no holidays, or, rather,
every day becomes a holiday),
for some years now.
So the 120 published titles
are only a small fraction of my work."

And I'm sure that he'd want to add this —
think twice, then twice again,
young man or young woman,
whose wildest, fondest dream
is becoming a poet,
of joining this priestly order.

Instead, try something easy
like being prime minister,
or single-handed blowing up the world.

65

T.O.

STATISTICS SHOW PHILLIES
FAVOURED TO TAKE IT ALL

"To hell with that" — Paul Mollitor,
tripling in the first,
homering in the third,
to lead the thirteen-hit barrage:
Jays 10, Phillies 3,
and a World Series lead
two games to one!

CHARLES OLSON AT THE FORD HOTEL

What was it about taking photographs
that put us off then — the awkward posing,
over-exposure to thick family albums
with twenty snapshots of Uncle Bill?

Whatever the reason,
we never got one of the great Charles Olson
lounging outside the Ford Hotel on Bay Street,
that afternoon of April 30, 1960,
only hours away from his first huge appearance
before the faithful at the Isaacs Gallery.

As it turned out, expert wreckers soon ripped down
that 600-room, twelve-bucks-a-night hotel,
in what seemed no time at all,
not too many dreary years later.
I've almost forgotten by now
what they threw up in its place —
the Atrium on Bay, I think,
with another fine old T.O. landmark,
the Lichee Garden, with great Chinese dining,
opening up in a ground-floor location,
after being dragged roughly from its moorings
on Chinatown's Elizabeth Street.

But, getting back to our friend, Charles Olson,
and the legend (partly rumour, partly fact),
that the one night he slept in the Ford
he at some point
gave a very hefty, stretching jab
while still very much in dreamland
(his 6' by 3' bed
not too great a fit
for a 6' 6" giant),
and slammed a mighty fist right through
what seemed like a cardboard inner wall
in his rinky-dink cubbyhole.

Which act, if you're buying the story,
shook the twin tower he was sleeping in
right to the very guts of its foundations,
so badly, we're told,
that when demolition day finally came,
the clever blasting engineer
used one third the regular charge
to bring that old mighty flea-bag
swiftly crashing deathward down.

NOVEMBER 24, 1992

November squats
on the ruins of the year
ready to shit out winter.

LEANER, MEANER

Sun, shine your strongest magic down
on these crowd-clustered faces
of my fellow-citizens,
gathered before the eroded pile
of our Queen's Park parliament,
not in anger, as it turns out,
but in bantering good-humour
with a tolerance for fools.

Now it's time for the right honourable
premier of this great province,
to slip on one
of his more boyish faces,
before he emerges on the platform
to address his fellow-Ontarians —
or "the Mob" — as I'm sure his bodyguards,
armed and ready for combat,
a human shield massed
in closed ranks around him,
most certainly think of them.

WHEN LACROSSE WAS KING

If you're a male
and under 95,
beginning May first
in this sixtieth year
of our dear Queen Victoria's reign,

all those capable of carrying
a lacrosse stick
or reasonable facsimile thereof,
are invited to ride free of charge
on any one of R.J. Fleming's
Toronto Street Railway trams.

Of course someone has to pay
for all this generosity —
and unfortunately that will be
all you other passengers,
who'll have to dig down deep
to come up with a quarter
for your next eight rides.

WINTER DEATH, BUS SHELTER

"Homeless man freezes to death in bus shelter" — Toronto
Star, January 6, 1996.

"We don't seem to have too much to say
as to when or where we're going to die,
but having once worked a whole summer
digging graves in Mount Pleasant Cemetery,
I've always thought of it
as the perfect place for a person
to lay themselves down for good,
especially under one of those white-flowering,
broad-leafed horse-chestnut trees,
at the start of the balmy summer season.

"So you can easily guess
that I wasn't exactly prepared
to die like a block of ice,
at four in the morning on a bench
in a draughty, stinking TTC bus shelter
at Spadina and Nassau Street,
with the temperature hovering around
a mind-destroying minus twenty Celsius,

"and for once when the two big, caring policemen
shook and shook me, I didn't move a muscle,
quite enjoying all my new-found privileges
of frozen death."

GO TOUCH TIMOTHY

When he's sure no-one's watching,
one nervous, all arms-and-legs student,
sidles up in his most innocent manner
to the eight-foot-high bronze sculpture
of our good Captain Timothy,
a man not too much at ease
in the solid-backed chair
the artist has put him in,
while the no-nonsense look in the face
makes his store's pledge quite believable:
"Goods satisfactory
or money refunded"
(not to worry,
we'll stiff our suppliers).

So Timothy sits there, back turned
to the grinding Yonge and Dundas
bedlam outside (a hawker's paradise),
no street noise to bother him
with the most modern
window-glass surrounding him,
sound-proof and all-serene as it must be
down the endless shopping aisles
of his flagship super-centre.

And it's now that our student
becomes bold at last, bends down to plant
his symbolic pinch on the bronze-booted
right foot of the esteemed,
stern-faced founder of the dynasty,
which action, or so the legend has it,
is guaranteed to bring the prankster
much the same kind of magic luck
as Timothy himself enjoyed
(after many years of anguish,
crushed hopes and desperate sweat, that is).

But all of this, if the evening papers,
those headline twisters, are to be believed,
may be coming to a quick, inglorious end,
as they crow time may soon be running out
for Ye Olde Firme, which smart insiders claim
has been blithely coasting toward the New Millennium
on a sleigh-run iced with unimaginative greed,
though heavily blessed with Ulster gall and guile;

and now before too long will have to turn,
face all its enemies head-on,
their innuendoes of bankruptcy
rising up like a chant in the bitter air.

All of which finally raises
the unanswerable question
for all loyal minds to ponder:
who will tell Timothy?

75

BLACK TRILLIUM

No-one noticed this one black trillium
growing quietly in St. Mark's Wood
among its white brothers,
its shy, even whiter sisters,

until suddenly it burst on the world,
every shiny black petal gleaming,
to spread a welcome veil of peace
across the battered face
of a despairing world,
in one great burst of song!

BLOOR-DANFORTH SUBWAY CAR

Much sooner than expected
a subway train glides in
(it's going to Kipling,
but I'm getting off at Jane),

and I'm only barely seated
when I see straight across from me,
neatly blocking the exit door,
the very same young couple
I thought I'd shaken for good,
after standing close to them
on the subway platform at Main.

Not exactly weirdos,
but still in some ways weird;
the young woman still daubing
at the nasty cut on her forehead
just above the right eye,
with a piece of blood-spotted Kleenex,
her close-to-beautiful face
showing more resignation than terror,
as she stands beside the young punk
with his crotch-tight jeans suggesting
even more menace than the expressionless face
too cool to show any weakness or emotion.

Now he starts in berating her
from the corners of those thin, hard lips:
"When that stupid little cut
has stopped bleeding, bitch,
I'll belt you even harder
on the other side, so you can't complain
I'm playing any favourites."

And I wonder if any passengers
on this subway car beside me,
wish him horrible instant death
beneath our train's crushing, slicing wheels?

Then finally, a little late, agreed,
but still soon enough to make my day —
the object of my disgust and hidden fear,
together with his pitiful
punching-bag of a girlfriend,
get off at Coxwell, taking those doomed faces
out of my life, O Lord, please forever.

MIKE WHITE AT THE WESTOVER

"Honest to God, one night
with a final, rousing trumpet chorus,
he lifted the hair-piece
of a guy clean off —
some boozer at a table
real close to the bandstand.

"But don't get me wrong,
he could lay down a ballad
like "I'm Through with Love,"
or maybe even "Sugar,"
with such a velvet-soft touch
that he reached the toughest heart,

"and each time it happened
in that crummy place,
it got so quiet you could hear
the damn flies buzzing overhead."

79

NIGHT OF THE HUNDRED BREADS

Lighting up their ovens for another shift,
baking bread for a hundred hungry races,
bread with a hundred different textures,
shapes, sizes; bakeries on Claremont,
Eglinton, College, Queen, and on how many
other streets, other neighbourhoods
I've never even heard of.

Ovens are quickly firing up
one by one, so whether it's *pain,*
pan, pane or *pão,* white, brown or pumpernickel,
raisin, egg-loaf or crusty French sticks,
dough shaped by many hands
awaits the ovens' heat, deft use of paddles
pushing it into place, the first tempting whiff
of the bread's fragrance rising — some of it wafted
into nearby streets, where passersby receive it
like a blessing, a chance act of love,
marked with the certain joy
of simple pleasures still alive and well
in this city of life-renewing earth.

MORE VIOLENCE ON THE PICKET LINE

Legislative Buildings, Queen's Park

When the law's fairly,
squarely settled within,
order will cease to be
a problem without.

When the roots of the law
shall be fondly watered,
civility will bloom again
like the overflowing flowerbeds of spring.

81

HIGH PARK CROSS-COUNTRY RUN

University of Toronto Schools, 1936

Bill and I did our best to handle it
like we thought two professionals would —
picking an October afternoon
a week or so before the big race,
to jog over what we thought would be
the route the school would chose
for its three-mile cross-country run.

This took us up and down
many winding footpaths on the hills
looking down on Grenadier Pond,
with a tough final stretch
going up the asphalt turnings
of a road beside the park's small zoo
with its fenced-in huts and cages,

then, with that conquered,
we stumbled on across the sports field
and the cricket pitch to the finish-line
not far from the Bloor Street pavilion,
its refreshment stand a very welcome sight
to two exhausted runners
still amazed that they were both on their feet.

Luckily, though, a week later,
when the day of the big race came,
I'd lost nearly all of my stiffness,
that is, until the first mile's dipsy-doodle
up and down those steep Grenadier slopes,
after which my legs and feet were dead weights
somehow still attached to my body.
And from then on it seemed that almost all
my two hundred fellow-sufferers in the race,
were passing me by, quickly vanishing
up and over the next weary hill.

So you can easily imagine
how I almost died of instant shock,
when, as I finally staggered over
what appeared to be the white-ribbon finish-line,
some joker grabbed me by the arm
and shouted, "Here's the novice winner!"

Minutes later I was still recovering
from leg pains, foot pains, out-of-breath pains,
half-slumped on a bench in the pavilion,
with minor bedlam still rising from the racers,
and Bill repeating the details of his sad, sad story,
while I tried to sip from the piping-hot mug of cocoa
the school had thoughtfully provided,
well aware it had a burnt smell and tasted funny,
but at least felt good going down,
and was helping me pretend
I'd finished up the race
in not too bad shape
for a rank beginner.

What next? First off,
I violently threw up
my burnt-cocoa drink,
then felt even worse
for the next half-hour.
But somehow got home,
took a steaming-hot bath,
and still ached in every muscle.

My prize as the novice winner of the race
was a shiny medal suitably inscribed,
which I lost not too long after.
And, believe it or not, I never ran
another cross-country race again,
or any other race for that matter;
and now sixty-odd years later,
I'm still left with the vivid memory
of that loathsome, burnt taste
of my cup of Baker's Cocoa.

ACTION CENTRAL

"If you want to let
more bloody insects into this room,
it's okay by me, honey-child."

But I doubt if she's kidding
anyone in the other cubicles
of this emergency ward —
they know that strident voice,
that high-on-drugs (or booze) wail.

What the hell do you expect
on a Saturday night,
at a Sunday School picnic?

85

Pictures from a Long-Lost World

PICTURES FROM A LONG-LOST WORLD:
JOHN BROWN LEADS A RAID ON THE ARSENAL
ON HARPERS FERRY, OCTOBER 16, 1859

PART ONE: THE PLAN

On first consideration, this choice
of a meeting-place and convention site
in the peaceful country town of Chatham, Canada
(slightly east of Michigan)
might have seemed a peculiar choice
for this strange gathering of Americans
from neighbouring Ohio;

but you had to remember that at the time,
Chatham, Ontario was the northern terminus
of the Underground Railway,
an organization deeply involved
in the escape of American slaves
to freedom in Canada.
And it was from the many ex-slaves
living in the area that the leader
of this new group seen about town
hoped to raise volunteers
for a startling new enterprise.

On the morning of May 8, 1858,
a meeting was held
of convention delegates.
The chairman of the meeting,
a certain Aaron D. Stevens,
introduced with a few well chosen words
a 59-year-old man, John Brown,
who, Stevens told the meagre audience,
had learned at his father's knee
to regard the enslavement of Negroes
as a great sin against God,
and had vowed eternal war against slavery.

With that a compactly built, wiry man stood up,
long milk-white beard waving in the wind,
his movements almost cat-like. He took
the few steps to the platform,
where he faced a small, attentive audience.
And while at first glance he might have appeared to some
as ageing or prematurely old,
all doubts faded as he began addressing them
in a vigorous, confident manner.
"My plan straight off,"
he told the eager faces before him,
"is to strike at a vulnerable point
somewhere in the South, then follow that up
with a giant slave uprising,
in which even free Negroes
in the Northern States and Canada
will flock to our support.
I'll lead my men into the mountains,
and if any hostile action should be taken
against us by the Separate States,
then most certainly we'll defeat
their spiritless militia
and, God willing, the army
of these wretched slave-owners."

The old guerrilla chief now sat down
to considerable applause, and shortly after
the meeting voted to accept his plan
by adopting a Provisional Constitution
and Related Ordinances, which
for the people of those states
would act as the law of the land,
while the army of liberation
formed a new government —
one that would not, of course, supplant
the Government of the United States,
but exist side by side with it,
and work to prohibit slavery.

John Brown was then elected
Commander-in-Chief of the Provisional Army
that would be formed, and other officers
were selected as well.
With that this Canadian convention
broke up, with most of Brown's group
scattering widely back
into the United States,
to look for some kind of work
until they were called upon
to march to Virginia.

Brown himself sent
a highly-trusted associate,
John E. Cook,
directly to Harpers Ferry,
a small town right on the border
of the slave State, Virginia,
which, because of the closeness of the mountains,
would provide a hiding-place for his men.
In addition it was only forty miles
from the free State of Pennsylvania
and the site of a US armoury and arsenal,
which was said to hold much-needed arms and ammunition.

Brown meanwhile had to plead his case
before the so-called Secret Six,
northern abolitionists who could give him
both moral and financial help.
At one stroke he gained
most of the money and weapons
he'd need to proceed with his attack.

Now it was time for Brown himself
to go to Harpers Ferry,
and on July 3, 1859,
together with two of his sons,
34-year-old Owen
and Oliver, a young man of 20,
as well as a Kansas veteran,
Jeremiah O. Anderson,

he entered the town to consult with
his man, John E. Cook,
who in one short year of residence
had no fewer than four occupations,
and had managed as well
to wed a local girl.
With Cook's expert help,
Brown and his three companions
found lodgings in a private home
in Sandy Hook, a mile or two down the Potomac
on the Maryland side,
where they passed themselves off
as Isaac Smith and Sons,
simple farmers on the lookout
for good farm land to develop.

Wasting no time
Brown was up early next morning,
eager to find a discreet hiding-place
for his band of raiders.
Friendly inquiries in the neighbourhood
led him to a farm five miles north
of Harpers Ferry, called the Kennedy Farm,
which he decided, though it was small,
because it was in an isolated area,
and surrounded by woods,
provided good opportunities for concealment
of both men and supplies.

To help keep the farm as free as possible
from local gossip, Brown asked his wife,
and his daughter as well,
to come and live with him there;
and although his wife
couldn't join him right away,
his daughter Annie and his son's wife Martha
arrived in mid-July, with their woman's touch
being put to immediate good use,
Martha doing the cooking
and helping Annie with the household chores.
As Brown had foreseen,
neighbours did drop in
from time to time unannounced,
even in such a remote location;
luckily, no suspicion seemed to be aroused,
though there were a few close calls.

With his base of operations now secured,
John Brown was ready
to press on with preparations
for the actual raid.
On July 10 he wrote
his lieutenant, John Kagi,
now at Chambersburg, Pennsylvania,
with an arms depot already set up,
giving him full directions for forwarding
both the men and the shipments of freight
(the freight in this case
being 200 Sharps rifles, 1000 pikes
and 200 pistols). These weapons,
well crated in strong wooden boxes,
marked very plainly "Hardware and Castings,"
were sent by rail from Ohio to Chambersburg,
then shipped by waggon to the Kennedy Farm
without a single hitch.

Next, alone or in twos and threes,
Brown's volunteers began to assemble
at the farm, which consisted of two log buildings,
some outbuildings and a pasture,
and as time went on
a small cabin near the house
was pressed into service,
as twenty or more active bodies
would eventually be jammed
into very close quarters.
Brown soon found the trick
was somehow to keep them all busy,
at the same time of course out of sight
through the daylight hours,
which was managed by playing cards
or checkers, reading magazines, telling stories

or arguing mightily
about politics or religion,
two sure-fire attention-getters
among these men
of such widespread backgrounds.
No doubt the freeing of the slaves
would have been their one area of agreement,
the single hope that united them all.

Other activities included frequent drilling,
the study of guerrilla warfare.
The men ate their meals
downstairs in the basement kitchen
of the old farmhouse, now bulging at the walls,
with the upstairs floor serving as a second kitchen,
parlour, dining-room, also doubling
as bedrooms, with the attic being used
as a drilling-space, storeroom
and general hiding-place,
every inch of the dwelling
being put to uses
never dreamed of by its former owners.

Luckily the main house was almost a hundred yards
back from the public road
connecting Harpers Ferry with Boonesborough
and Sharpsburg, Maryland,
so the men could go out after dark
for fresh air and exercise.
These occasions helped release
some of the pressures of close confinement,
but before long Brown saw his men
were close to the end of the rope —
indeed, twice there was almost a revolt
against going ahead with their plan;
and here Brown showed his leadership abilities
by each time tendering his resignation
immediately, then only withdrawing it
after getting a new vote of confidence
from all his followers.

With the coming of October,
the date of the attack
finally settled and drawing near,
Brown immediately put his men to work
overhauling pistols, checking rifles,
as well as attaching pike-heads
to iron shafts — no fewer than a thousand
two-edged dirks were made, with an iron blade
eight inches long attached to a six-foot ash handle,
which Brown reasoned, with considerable logic,
that put in the hands of freed slaves
with no knowledge of firearms,
together with the rifles of his trained men,
could give a good account of themselves
in any hand-to-hand combat with the enemy.

97

In the meantime, the American
Secretary of War, John B. Floyd,
had received an unsigned letter reporting
the existence of a secret organization,
having as its objective the liberation
of the southern slaves
in a general insurrection,
and having as its immediate target
"an Armoury in Maryland."
John Brown was named as its leader,
and if the unknown informant hadn't erred
in making the location Maryland
instead of Virginia, and if the Secretary hadn't thought
the report complete nonsense and filed it
carelessly away, history might have taken
quite a different turn.

Brown, meanwhile, still hung back
even with October arriving,
hopeful of more recruits
to swell his meagre ranks.
The truth was, however,
that many who'd promised to join
now hung back for many reasons,
even two of his sons,
Jason and Salmon,
decided against taking part.
So, with the welcome arrival
of three more recruits,
John Brown decided
his waiting should come to an end;
he couldn't risk waiting any longer,
to be thwarted now would be unbearable,
his life's utter ruin.

His Provisional Army
of the United States
now comprised 22 men
besides himself as Commander-in-Chief;
of these, nineteen were under thirty,
three not yet twenty-one.
Gathering his force together,
Brown announced that the attack
would take place the following night,
October 16, and he cautioned them all
very seriously about the needless taking
of human life.
"You all know how dear life is to you,
then consider that the lives of others
are every bit as dear to them.
Do not therefore take the life of anyone
if you can possibly avoid it.
But if it is necessary to take life
in order to save your own,
then make short work of it."

The next day, Sunday,
October 16, 1859,
was a quiet one for the men,
the morning starting out
with a service of worship led by Brown,
during which he noticed how his men's mood
had changed to one of "deep solemnity."
The volunteers then sat down
as a body for breakfast, with a roll-call
following afterwards. They then received
their last instructions:
everything was now ready,
their fate and their cause
solely in the hands of God.

The rest of that day
seemed endless to everyone.
So it was almost with relief
that Brown addressed his raiders at 8 PM,
gently yet firmly. "Men," he told them,
"shoulder your arms; we will proceed to the Ferry."
And with that short command
the men slung their precious Sharps rifles
over their shoulders, where they were hidden
under long grey shawls,
which doubled as overcoats,
then stood in line waiting
for the order to march.
A horse and waggon were led
quickly out into the yard,
with a few stores in back to be used
later that night — a sledge-hammer,
several pikes and a crowbar.
Three men were then detailed
to stay behind at the farm,
form a rear-guard; in the morning
they'd bring the rest of the weapons
close to the town, where it was hoped
they'd be handed to those breakaway slaves
John Brown was counting on
to swell his slender force of 22.

Then Brown himself appeared,
wearing a battered Kansas cap,
which had seen him safely through
countless frontier skirmishes, close escapes,
and slowly mounted the waggon, took the reins,
at the same time giving
the signal to move out,
first down the farmhouse lane,
then onto the Maryland road,
with Harpers Ferry a five-mile march away.

The men marched in silence as they pleased,
mostly in twos and threes,
a strange collection of five blacks
and fourteen whites (made smaller still
by the absence of the three-man rearguard),
lawyer marching alongside farmer,
escaped convict side by side
with Quaker and spiritualist,
former slave and petty drifter,
now united in one common bond,
a deep-felt hatred of slavery,
each man quite prepared to die
to free the slaves once and for all.
A few John Brown had met in "bleeding Kansas,"
where they had their first taste of war,
but most volunteers would fight tonight
for the very first time,
with only a limited chance
to study guerrilla tactics
or other fighting skills.

So it was only fitting
that his young son Oliver,
who claimed he was his father's
personal bodyguard; Charlie Tidd,
former Maine woodsman and very close friend
of Brown's from the Kansas cavalry,
together with John Cook, Yale student
and New York law apprentice
before joining Brown in bloody Kansas,
should be the first to follow close behind
that creaking, rattling old waggon
which had riding up top the man
who'd brought them through safe so far,
three comrades Brown knew he could count on
to be close behind wherever fate might lead.
But for now he ordered Tidd and Cook,
both of whom knew the country around them,
to reconnoitre the winding road ahead,
although he thought the chances were small
of meeting someone dangerous at night.

Next, moving very easily close behind,
one of the main group, Aaron Stevens,
professional soldier, a former colonel
with the Second Kansas
Regiment of Volunteers.
a tower of strength in the group,
marched beside John Kagi,
school-teacher, lawyer,
still recovering from wounds
suffered while out riding hard
with Stevens' Second Kansas boys.
Right behind them marched
two rows of raw recruits,
none of whom had yet taken
any active roles in the anti-slavery cause,
but were all staunch abolitionists,
drawn by Brown's magnetic example
of God-fearing leadership —
Watson Brown, 24, accompanied by not one
but two brothers and two neighbours;
William and Dauphin Thompson, 26 and 20,
the latter never having been away
from home before; following behind them,
Albert Hazlitt, at 22 a Kansas veteran,
and Canadian-born Stewart Taylor,
23 years old, a former waggon-maker
and spiritualist, with a premonition
he'd die at Harpers Ferry;
then came Edwin Coppoc, 24, a year older
than his brother Barclay (now serving as rearguard
at the farm with Owen Brown and Francis Meriam),
both brothers staunch Quakers who'd been in Kansas
while the fighting raged, but had taken no part
in the conflict; then finally joined with John Brown
a year before in Iowa.

With them strode William H. Leeman,
a New Englander from Maine,
who'd worked in a shoe factory there,
and walking at their side
20-year-old Oliver,
John Brown's youngest son,
still wondering why his two older brothers
had decided not to serve, while he'd already fought
in his father's outfit,
the Kansas Liberty Guards, an impulsive youngster
"blessed with a good intellect, great ingenuity."

After that group came Dangerfield Newby,
a 44-year-old mulatto born a slave
but freed by his loving Scots father;
and next to him another free Negro,
Osborn P. Anderson,
who'd worked as a printer in Canada,
before joining John Brown in '58;
he had a wife and several children
still slaves in the South, and was certain
that the only way they'd ever be freed
was with rifle and bullet in determined hands.
And beside these two serious believers
tramped "Emperor" Shields Green,
an illiterate escaped slave
from South Carolina, and bringing up the rear
of this small company of men,
two latecomers who'd arrived
just the day before, and would complete
the ranks of this Provisional Army
of the United States — John Copeland,
an Ohio Negro, and his friend Lewis Leary, both 25,
making 23 men, including the Commander-in-Chief,
not nearly enough for their ambitious plan,
but Brown felt he couldn't wait another day.

And so the short march to Harpers Ferry
continued on, the tiny force now glad
of their long grey shawls, with a chilling
night wind at their backs;
and if they'd thought to look up,
they'd have seen the drizzle of rain
around the Blue Ridge Mountains
reaching up all around them.
For a few short minutes now
these men had time to reflect
on this turn of events in their lives;
many had no doubts at all
how they'd fare in the impending skirmish,
with those who had never been in combat
wondering how they'd measure up
to their baptism of fire.
And, as they neared the end
of the two-hour march,
they could imagine their scouts,
Charlie Tidd and John Cook, would be busy
cutting telegraph lines on both sides
of the broad Potomac,
and suddenly they all felt ready
for almost anything, after this marching
in silence on a lonely, misty country road.

Finally, at 10.30 PM,
they reached the railway bridge
of the Baltimore and Ohio Railway,
better known as the B. and O.,
which was a long, wooden-roofed structure
spanning the Potomac River
slightly upstream from the point
where the Shenandoah River
comes flowing in majestically from the south.
John Brown's plan now called
for Kagi and Stevens,
that trusty, experienced pair,
to enter the dark cavern of the bridge,
follow the railway tracks quickly through it,
then come out in sight of the building
that housed the railroad depot and the Wager Hotel —
and everything went as planned.
Not far from the tunnel entrance,
the two scouts met a railroad watchman
coming cautiously toward them holding a lantern,
no doubt quite surprised
to have company on his night shift.
He was quickly taken aback
without a shot being fired,
and at this point John Brown turned
horse and waggon onto the bridge,
with all but two soldiers
(detailed as a rear-guard),
of this pitifully small Provisional Army
of the United States
following close behind it,
while hurriedly affixing cartridge boxes
to the outside of their clothing
for speedy access once the fight began.

And now after taking only a few minutes
to make the dark ultimate crossing,
the raiders emerged from the eerie blackness
of the B. and O. covered bridge
into a silent, sleeping town
with empty, inviting streets.
John Brown could plainly see before him
the large building that did double duty
as both a railway depot and a hotel,
and just beyond that, to the left,
the grey, indistinct mass
of the United States Arsenal buildings,
where he knew many thousands of guns were stored,
awaiting the liberators. Finally, to his right
the Armoury shops stretching in a double row
all along the Potomac.
There was not an instant's hesitation now:
with a quick pull on the reins,
John Brown turned horse and waggon
toward the waiting armoury —
riding at that moment
straight into history.

*For John Brown and the six survivors of the raid on Harpers
Ferry, death came by hanging after a trial by jury.
But John Brown's words, written shortly before his execution
on December 2, 1859, would not wait long to be fulfilled:
"I, John Brown, am now quite certain that the crimes of this
guilty land will never be purged away but with blood. I had,
as I now think, flattered myself that without very
much bloodshed it might be done." But by February 1, 1861,
seven southern States had formed the Confederate States
of America at Montgomery, Alabama. Before many months
would pass soldiers in Union blue would be marching toward
the South to the tune of "John Brown's Body."*

RAYMOND SOUSTER is one of Canada's best-known poets. He began his career before the end of the war and won the Governor General's Award, for *The Colour of the Times*, in 1964. He moved to Oberon five years later and has now published thirteen titles under our imprint., as well as eight volumes of *Collected Poems*. This is his most recent book.